Conrad Elroy, Powder Monkey
The Role of the Navy in the Civil War

Alvin Robert Cunningham

Perfection Learning®

To the loving memory of my late mother, Lorene Cunningham, and younger brother, Pete Cunningham

Editorial Director: Susan C. Thies
Editor: Mary L. Bush

Cover Design: Michael A. Aspengren
Book Design: Deborah Lea Bell and Emily Greazel
Image Research: Lisa Lorimor

Photo Credits: Museum of the Confederacy, Richmond Virginia; p. 5; Northwind Picture Archives: pp. 16, 18–19, 24 (bottom), 25 (top), 26, 30 (top), 30–31 (top), 34–35, 41

ArtToday (www.arttoday.com): pp. 2, 7 (bottom), 11 (top), 16–17 (bkgd), 25 (bkgd), 29 (bottom), 36–37 (bkgd); CMOHS, Congressional Medal of Honor Society: p. 44; ©Digital Stock: pp. 2–3, 4, 8, 9 (bottom, bkgd), 10 (top), 11 (bottom), 10–11 (bkgd), 12–13 (bottom, bkgd), 14–15, 15 (top), 16–17, 18–19 (bkgd), 20–21 (bkgd), 22–23, 24 (top), 28–29 (center, bkgd), 29 (top), 30–31 (bkgd), 32 (left), 34 (top), 35, 38, 39, 42 (top), 43 (bkgd), 45 (top), 48 (top); Library of Congress: cover, pp. 1, 6 (bottom-left), 7 (top), 10 (bottom), 32 (center), 33, 36–37, 40, 42–43; Massachusetts Commandery Military Order of the Loyal Legion and the US Army Military History Institute: pp. 6–7; NAIL: pp. 26–27 (bkgd), 30 (bottom), 40–41 (bkgd); Tobi Cunningham: pp. 12, 33, 34, 35, 37, 44–48 (bkgd)

Text © 2003 **Perfection Learning® Corporation**.
All rights reserved. No part of this book may be reproduced, stored in a retrieval system, or transmitted in any form or by any means, electronic, mechanical, photocopying, recording, or otherwise, without prior permission of the publisher. Printed in the United States of America.

For information, contact
Perfection Learning® Corporation
1000 North Second Avenue, P.O. Box 500
Logan, Iowa 51546-0500.
Phone: 1-800-831-4190 • Fax: 1-800-543-2745
perfectionlearning.com

1 2 3 4 5 BA 06 05 04 03 02

ISBN 0-7891-5851-5

Contents

Shelling destroyed huge areas of land in both the North and the South.

The Potter House in Atlanta was damaged but still standing after General William Sherman took the city on September 2, 1864.

INTRODUCTION

THE Civil War was the bloodiest and most devastating war in American history. From 1861 to 1865, huge American armies crossed the country making war on each other. Private homes became army headquarters. Churches and schools became temporary hospitals. Americans slaughtered other Americans on American land. American troops destroyed American cities and towns.

This terrible war claimed 620,000 American lives. That is more than the combined deaths of all the other American wars. At the time, the country's population was only 30 million. That means that 1 out of every 50 Americans was killed in this war. It also means that 1 out of every 12 men and boys between the ages of 15 and 50 were killed. Also, more than half the soldiers who were not killed were either wounded or taken prisoner.

Why the War?

The cause of the war was long-coming and complicated. Its roots went back to the birth of America, where slavery was protected in the Constitution. The northern and southern parts of the United States had different geographies and climates. As a result, they developed rival economies and lifestyles. Over time, this helped shape the United States government and laws. It also helped put the North and South on a collision course.

Since the early 1800s, the North had enjoyed the prosperity of the **Industrial Revolution**. With good waterways, Northern cities like New York, Boston, and Chicago became centers of business and industry. By the 1850s, manufactured goods were being shipped throughout the world. Immigrants came to the United States to work in the Northern mines, mills, shipyards, and factories. Northerners believed that with intelligence and hard work, every person had a chance to make a fortune.

The South, however, was not as affected by the Industrial Revolution. It kept its rural character and agricultural economy based on cash crops, such as cotton, rice, tobacco, and sugar. These crops were grown on large farms called *plantations*, owned by powerful, wealthy families.

Plantations depended almost entirely on black slaves for their labor force. These slaves worked from sunrise to sunset. They lived in run-down shanties and were not allowed to leave the plantation. Black slaves were bought, sold, and traded like livestock. Many were treated more like animals than humans. Plantation owners owed their wealth and power to this cheap slave labor.

Once the war began, many slaves ran away to join the Union's fight to end slavery. These slaves were called *contraband*.

Most Northerners viewed slavery and the plantation system as economic evils. More and more, issues concerning slavery came between the two sides. Would the new western territories allow slavery? How could the South stop the North from helping runaway slaves? These questions threatened to tear the **Union** apart.

Many Southerners didn't own slaves, but they still feared that the more populated North would take control of the national government. Then it could pass laws that would destroy their Southern way of life.

Outbursts of violence over these issues occurred in the government and throughout the country. The presidential election of 1860 brought the crisis to a head. Southerners believed that if Abraham Lincoln was elected, their property (including slaves) and society would be destroyed forever.

To Stay or Go?

Lincoln's victory was the point of no return for most Southerners. They felt that the majority of Northerners did not respect the Constitution's protection of slavery. So they believed they had no choice but to secede, or leave, the Union. Southerners also felt they had a legal right and a moral duty to start their own country.

In contrast, the Northerners felt that **secession** was illegal. They believed that the Union should not be divided. They also felt that secession was an open rebellion against the government.

South Carolina was the first state to secede. Ten other Southern states soon followed. Their new country was called the Confederate States of America. Jefferson Davis was its president.

For Honor and Beliefs

The actual collision between the North and South took place on April 12, 1861. The Confederate forces of South Carolina fired on Fort Sumter in Charleston Harbor. In time, the Union forces in Fort Sumter had to surrender. This was the beginning of the bloodiest war in American history.

Abraham Lincoln

The Civil War was fought by two parties of unequal strength. The industrial North had many more resources for making war materials. They also had a much larger fighting population. The agricultural South was always at a disadvantage. So after four long years, the **Confederacy** was forced to admit defeat due to a shortage of food, clothing, and war materials. They were not defeated for lack of courage. Both sides fought bravely. And both the North and the South were willing to risk it all for their honor and beliefs.

This book's historical fiction chapters tell the story of Conrad Elroy, a powder monkey who displayed courage aboard the U.S.S *Hartford* at the battle of Mobile Bay.

The nonfiction chapters explain the important role that the Union and Confederate **navies** played in the Civil War.

Fort Sumter was left in ruins after the Union forces surrendered.

The Plan

"Kneel down and grab those **bibles**, **powder monkeys**," barked the **master-at-arms**. "This gun deck needs to be **holystoned** again!"

Conrad Elroy studied the man's red face and the bulging vein in his neck.

"We've been coaling up since morning, and this ship's mighty dirty."

Powder Monkey

A powder monkey's main job was to supply gunpowder to the gun crews.

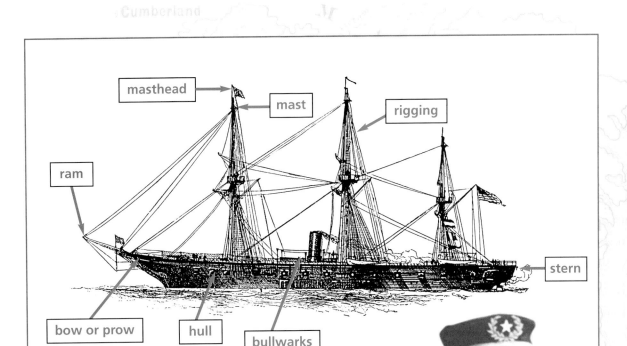

Conrad watched him walk to the rail and point toward shore.

"That's Mobile Bay," he said, turning and looking down at the boys. "Maybe tomorrow, this **fleet** will sail in and take it from the **Rebs**!"

Conrad heard some clapping and cheers for the Union.

"All you boys have the honor of serving on the U.S.S. *Hartford*, the **flagship** of Admiral Farragut," he said. "You'll want to sail into battle with your colors flying above a clean ship. So let's get scrubbing!"

Conrad Elroy felt sick. He was fed up with that man ordering him around. And he was tired of doing servant's work for the past two months. He stared at the bucket of hot water that he'd carried up from the engine room's **boiler**. His sore, callused hands poured some on the wooden deck. The coal dust changed to an inky liquid.

Admiral David G. Farragut

Colors Flying

When ships sail into battle, they raise the flag that represents their country or side. When the United States goes to war against another country, the U.S. flag is flown. In the Civil War, the Union flew the U.S. flag. The Confederacy created a new flag to represent their side. The North and the South flew their flags, or "colors," proudly during the war.

Then he picked up the Bible-sized chunk of sandstone with both hands. Reluctantly, he joined the other boys. His body rocked back and forth in the familiar scrubbing rhythm. Disturbing memories whirled in his head.

A young Union officer appeared in Conrad's mind. The soldier had visited his private school in Boston. Conrad remembered how all the girls had gathered around the soldier, admiring his new uniform. The principal had introduced the officer to his seventh-grade class as a graduate who was proudly serving his country.

Conrad had been jealous of the soldier and his uniform. It was then that he had gotten his idea. *He* could come to school wearing a new blue uniform too. Then all the girls would gather around *him*, and no one would tease him about his small size. His plan would show them all!

Conrad blinked back to the present. He poured more water on the deck and continued scrubbing. In no time, his mind was back at his family's mansion on Beacon Hill.

On that day, he had waited for his father to return from the factory he owned and for his mother to dismiss the servants. Then he had insisted that his parents sign the papers for him to enlist in the U.S. Navy. It could be their thirteenth birthday present to their only child. After all, they had promised to get him anything that his heart desired.

Conrad stopped scrubbing and looked around the ship. He saw that the U.S.S. *Hartford* really was preparing for battle.

Above the scraping sounds of the holystoning, he heard the ship's **marines** in drill. He recognized the rattling sounds of their muskets and sabers.

From his kneeling position, he saw the legs of gun crews. He could smell the cleaning oil they were applying to their cannons. Conrad watched seamen carrying medical supplies to the surgeons on the lower deck. Battle flags were taken from their cases.

Fear began to chew at Conrad's stomach. As a powder monkey for the **starboard** number three gun, he'd experienced many drills and firing practices. But his gun crew had only shot at flour barrels floating in the water. No cannons had been shooting back at them!

Conrad Elroy's plan was falling apart. He wasn't supposed to be scrubbing floors or going into battle. His father had promised that a friend in the Navy Department would arrange light duty for him. He was supposed to have a safe position and be treated better than the other young boys.

Gun crew on the deck of the *Hunchback*

"Elroy," snarled the Master-at-Arms, "get back to scrubbing or I'll have you climbing that **masthead** 'til the evening **mess**!"

Conrad didn't look up. He continued working in silence. Even though he was the smallest, he could climb the masthead and run faster than all the other powder monkeys. But that didn't seem to matter now. All he wanted was to get off that ship and get back home!

A Few Words About War Weapons

- A cannon is a large, heavy gun, usually attached to the deck of a ship.
- A musket is a heavy gun carried on the shoulder.
- A saber is a sword with a curved blade.

Honor Not the War, but the Warrior

"You can bring us another pot of coffee when you get a chance."

Conrad waved back to his gun captain. The officer and his crew were sitting around the **sailcloth** on the **berth** deck. After drying the metal cup, Conrad placed it back in the chest with the other utensils. Then he checked the **Mess Bill**. He saw that his name was listed as the cook's assistant.

Conrad glanced back at his gun crew and realized that something was different. Normally, when the drum called them for evening mess, the men would be talking and laughing and comparing letters they'd received from their mail call. But this evening, they were strangely quiet.

He carried the pot of coffee over and set it in the middle of the sailcloth. He noticed that some of the men were writing letters or reading Bibles. Others gave him a quick smile and continued smoking their pipes.

Walking back to the cooking area, Conrad was confused. One part of him was angry for being stuck on a navy ship that might be going into battle. That part of him wanted to run away. But the other part felt attached to his gun crew. These 14 men had always been kind to him.

They'd helped him become a better powder boy. They were like a second family to Conrad. That part of him wanted to stay and fight for the Union.

"Worried?"

Conrad looked up at Seaman Josh Pike, the gun crew's cook and powder handler. Josh was also his best friend on the ship.

"I guess," Conrad answered, looking back at his gun crew.

"The **scuttlebutt** is that we may attack Mobile Bay tomorrow. The crew always gets quiet before a possible battle," Josh explained. "Some men write letters to their loved ones back home. Others make peace with their God in case they don't survive."

Conrad looked up at his friend. "I've never been in a real battle before."

Josh put his hand on Conrad's shoulder. "I know," he said. "Come to my hammock after the evening inspection. Then we can talk about it."

"I'll be there," said Conrad. He watched Josh walk toward the other end of the berth deck.

☼ ☼ ☼

The *Hunchback* was originally a New York ferryboat.

Much later, the inspection of the guns and stations had been completed. Conrad carried his hammock bag from the main **bulwarks** and took it down to the berth deck. It was wet from the evening rain. Quickly he unpacked it and prepared it for sleep. Then he left and went looking for Josh.

"Conrad, come over here. I have some news." It was Ordinary Seaman Ben Davis, his gun crew's **sponger**. Conrad had gotten to know and trust this ex-slave. Ben and his family had managed to escape to the North with the help of the Underground Railroad.

The Confederate ram *Arkansas* alongside th Union gunboat *Carondelet*

When the war broke out, Ben immediately joined the Union navy to fight for his country.

Once, Ben had stood up for Conrad when an older powder boy had been bullying him. Conrad had always been grateful.

At that moment, Josh walked over and joined them.

"Our fleet is now complete," Ben explained. "The last wooden ship and **monitor** have just arrived."

"Any orders from the **admiral**?" asked Josh.

"Our captain just got the word. We'll be attacking tomorrow," answered Ben. "And **reveille** is at 2:00 a.m."

"Listen, Ben," said Josh, "Conrad and I are going to sit on my sea chest and have a short talk. Do you want to join us?"

"No," he answered, "I have to finish a letter to my family. **Tattoo** might come early tonight, and I can't write in the dark."

Conrad watched Ben leave and then followed his friend to his sea chest.

"Now, because you haven't been in battle before," explained Josh, "our gun captain has given me special permission to watch out for you."

"What do you mean?" asked Conrad.

The United States steamer *Mississippi* attempting to run down the Confederate ram *Manassas*

The Confederate cruiser C.S.S. *Alabama*

"I mean that you and I will work together in this battle. I'll tell you when to fetch powder cartridges from the **hatch**. Then you'll bring them right back to me and stay close."

Josh put his arm around Conrad's shoulder. "You'll have to be very brave tomorrow. Try to block out all the bad things that you see happening. Just focus on being a good powder boy for our gun crew. A lot of people will be counting on you."

"I hate the Rebs," Conrad mumbled, feeling scared inside.

"I can't think like that," said Josh. "My side of the Pike family moved north years ago, but I still have family in the Mobile area. Now they are fighting for what they believe is right—just like we are. We have to respect them for their courage. We must remember to honor not the war, but the warrior."

Conrad left and went back to his hammock. Trying to understand Josh's words made it difficult to fall asleep.

Confederate blockade-runner with a Union cruiser in the distance

Be a Man Today

At 2:00 a.m. on August 5, 1864, a loud bugle blew reveille and awakened Conrad. He sat up suddenly, nearly falling out of his hammock.

"Show a leg!" a voice shouted. "There's a general **muster** on the top deck. Store your hammocks first, and then report to your gun stations!"

Conrad stood on the berth deck, still groggy from sleep. All around him, men started unhooking and rolling up their hammocks. They talked among themselves.

Conrad's body shook as he rolled up his hammock and lashed it with the rope. After dressing quickly, he carried his hammock bag to the deck and stored it in the **rails** atop the main bulwarks. Then he followed the lantern light to the starboard number three gun.

"Conrad, I have some hot coffee and hardtack for you," said Josh. "It will help hold you 'til breakfast."

"Breakfast?"

"That's right," explained Josh. "Admiral Farragut told his staff that we'd be eating breakfast at 8:00 a.m. inside Mobile Bay."

"Do you think we can do it?"

"Listen, I was with him when he ran the guns at the battles of Vicksburg and New Orleans," answered Josh. "I believe he can get our fleet past the guns of Fort Morgan. And after we take Mobile Bay, it'll be the end of the **blockade-runners** getting out to the Gulf of Mexico. Then maybe this horrible war will end sooner!"

After they had finished their coffee and biscuits, they spent the next few hours helping prepare the U.S.S. *Hartford* for battle. They put up splinter nets on the starboard side. Then they barricaded the wheel and **steersmen** with sails and hammocks.

"We're protecting against wood splinters," explained Josh. "If a cannonball blows a hole in the side of our ship, chunks of wood will fly in all directions. I've seen sailors wounded and even killed by them."

They continued by laying sandbags on the deck over the steam machinery to help prevent fires from starting. Hanging **sheet chains** over the starboard side would help protect it from cannonballs.

"Hey, shrimp!" growled a deep voice. "You'd better stay out of my way today!"

Conrad studied the face that appeared in the light. It was the older powder boy from starboard number four gun.

U.S.S. or C.S.S. ?

The abbreviation U.S.S. stands for United States Ship. C.S.S. means Confederate States Ship. These titles identified which side the ship belonged to.

A Union victory at Mobile Bay would prevent blockade-runners from reaching the Gulf of Mexico.

"You're no 4 feet 8 inches tall. You're too short to be in this navy." His mean face stared down at Conrad's. "If you get in my way during the battle today, I'll stomp all over you!"

Then the face disappeared.

"Conrad, come over here!" yelled Josh.

Conrad walked over to his friend, trying not to show his fear.

"It's getting light now. The fleet is forming up," said Josh. "But before we go over and help, I want to remind you of something very important."

Conrad stepped closer.

"When you fetch a powder cartridge from the **magazine** hatch, make sure you put it in the leather pouch and close the top. In a battle, fires can break out. If the cartridge ever starts to burn, it will explode."

"I understand," said Conrad.

They went over and helped lash the U.S.S. *Metacomet* to the **port** side of their ship. Josh explained that this smaller wooden ship would act as a **tug** if the U.S.S. *Hartford* was shot up. Then he showed Conrad the five pairs of wooden ships behind them and the one pair in front. He also pointed out their four **ironclad** monitors and the **channel** they'd have to go through. Lastly, he showed him Fort Morgan with its 47 cannons.

Soon, all the gun crews were sent back to their stations.

"When we pass in front of the fort, we'll give her our starboard **broadsides**," explained Josh when they reached their station. "All our ships will. Then we'll deal with the ironclad **ram**, the C.S.S. *Tennessee*, when we get into the bay."

The *St. Louis* was the first ironclad gunboat built in America.

Josh pulled his friend close and looked into his eyes. "You're like a son to me, Conrad. I know you're still a boy, but today you must be a man." Then he pulled him even closer. "Do you understand me? Today you must be a man!"

Conrad nodded awkwardly. Then they both heard the first cannon shot from their lead monitor, the U.S.S. *Tecumseh*.

"Okay, Conrad, the battle has started," declared Josh.

Conrad Elroy could neither speak nor move. His body was frozen in fear!

Medal of Honor

"Conrad? Conrad?" Josh shook his friend's shoulder. "Stay focused and listen to what I tell you."

Conrad looked up at Josh and tried to clear his mind.

"The whole ship's preparing for battle," said Josh. "We'll be reaching Fort Morgan shortly."

"Hoist those American flags!" shouted the ship's captain. He pointed to the top of the **masts**.

Conrad glanced toward Captain Drayton and Admiral Farragut. They were standing near the main mast, looking up. Sailors were running to their posts. Gun captains were yelling orders to their crews.

"Battle stations!" yelled his gun captain.

Josh grabbed Conrad and pushed him out of the way of his crew. They were forming up around the cannon. "Now remember what I told you about the powder cartridges and doing your duty!" shouted Josh.

"Yes," answered Conrad, trying to calm himself.

"Now fetch our first powder cartridge." Josh handed him the leather container.

Conrad took it and started running toward the magazine hatch. His body was thawed out now. He maneuvered himself easily along the familiar route. When he reached the magazine,

U.S.S. *Brooklyn*

Admiral Farragut commanding his troops at Mobile Bay

the hatch door was open. He headed straight down the flight of stairs and joined the other powder boys.

"Quiet everyone!" ordered the seaman in front of the powder opening. "I don't want anyone talking. Come up orderly, get your cartridge, and get back to your guns. Now move!"

When it was his turn, Conrad stepped up and reached through the wet cloth. He placed the cartridge he was given in the container and closed the lid. Then he ran back to the number three gun and handed it to Josh.

BOOM! BOOM! BOOM!

"It's the U.S.S. *Brooklyn* firing on the fort!"

BOOM! BOOM! BOOM!

"See the smoke? It's the fort's guns." Josh pointed in that direction. "It's our turn next. Fetch another cartridge."

Before he could leave, the captain gave an order. "Load number three cannon!"

The U.S.S. *Hartford* collides with the C.S.S. *Tennessee.*

Conrad started running and didn't look back. He knew what his crew was doing. He'd watched them many times in their practice drills. When he reached the magazine landing, he waited quietly in the powder boy line.

"Something's wrong!" announced the seaman. "Our ship has stopped moving!"

BOOM! BOOM!

Conrad felt the floor vibrate.

"Our ship's being fired on. The fort's guns are reaching us!"

Then the seaman climbed to the top of the stairs and looked out.

BOOM! BOOM! BOOM! BOOM!

"Boys!" he shouted. "We're taking a terrible pounding. There's a lot of smoke and wood flying. Be careful going back!"

Conrad got his cartridge and climbed to the top of the stairs. He was shocked at the sight before him. Gun smoke was everywhere. Men were shouting and screaming in pain. Cannonballs were blasting through the sides of the ship. Wood chunks were flying everywhere.

Damage to the south side of Fort Morgan following the Battle of Mobile Bay

Conrad ran. He was almost to his cannon when he slipped and fell in a pool of blood. Then someone's hand reached down and pulled him up. It was Ben Davis.

"Help me drag this body to the port side."

Conrad looked down and saw that it was Josh, covered with blood. "But—but it's Josh," he stammered. "I can't do it!"

"Just grab him and help me!" BOOM! BOOM! "It's not Josh anymore. It's just a body now. So hurry up!"

Conrad helped drag Josh to the port side of the ship. They laid him with the other dead sailors. Conrad didn't want to leave. He just stood there looking down at his friend.

Then Ben took the gunpowder cartridge and gave Conrad the container. "Get us another one!"

Conrad felt sick and staggered only ten feet before throwing up. After he wiped his mouth, he remembered Josh telling him that he had to be a man today. So he held back the tears and ran down to the magazine landing.

"Get out of my way!" It was the number four gun powder boy, carrying a powder cartridge.

"Where's your container?" asked Conrad.

The powder boy didn't answer. He just ran up the stairs. Conrad quickly got his powder and caught up with the boy near gun number four. Suddenly, the ship lurched and the bully fell. His cartridge went sliding.

Conrad handed his gunpowder to Ben and stepped back. He could see where the boy's cartridge had slid. It had landed in a small fire near his gun crew. Because of the smoke that hung close to the deck, no one could see it except Conrad.

Everything seemed to slow down around him. He watched the gunpowder cartridge start to burn. He thought about Josh and the safety of his gun crew. Then Conrad found himself running to the burning cartridge. He picked it up with both hands and tried to throw it over the side of the ship.

BOOM!

Everything went black.

✳ ✳ ✳

It was a month after his medical **discharge** when Conrad's parents showed him the letter. It was from the U.S. government. It informed him that he had earned the Congressional Medal of Honor for his heroism aboard the U.S.S. *Hartford*. It was signed by Admiral Farragut and President Lincoln.

"Your principal has sent you an invitation to come to your school. They're having a war rally. All the students know about your medal," his father said proudly.

"And all the girls would really like to see you in your uniform," his mother added.

Conrad felt Josh's arm around him. "Tell the principal I won't be there."

He knew now that no uniform or medal was worth the cost of losing a friend. He had been a man. He had honored not the war, but the warrior. Now it was time to honor his friend.

Jefferson Davis was the president of the Confederacy.

Blockade-Runners and Commerce Raiders

The news of the fall of Fort Sumter spread quickly throughout the country. It brought wild rejoicing and waves of patriotism in both the North and the South. Lincoln and Davis called for volunteers to serve in the military for only three months. Both leaders felt that this conflict would not last very long. Young men on both sides responded with enthusiasm. Many were worried that the war would be over before they got to do any fighting.

The Southern attack on Fort Sumter was the beginning of the Civil War.

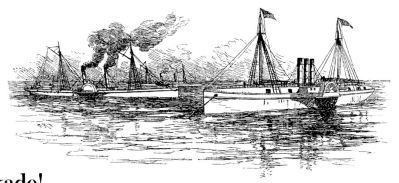

Blockade!

Lincoln talked with his military leaders. They knew the South would have to trade its cotton to other countries for war materials. Their plan was to create a complete naval **blockade** of the Southern states. This would prevent Southern ships from leaving their ports. In time, this plan would strangle the South into giving up. It was called the Anaconda Plan, named for the South American snake that kills its prey by strangling it.

Gideon Welles was the Union secretary of the navy. It would be his responsibility to create and maintain the blockade. In order to achieve that goal, he greatly expanded the navy. This was done in record time because of the industrial power of the North.

When the war broke out, the Confederates took control of the federal coastal forts. The North then had to launch combined naval and army **maneuvers** to take them back. In addition, the Union planned to take control of the Mississippi River. Then they would attack and capture the Confederate capitol at Richmond, Virginia.

Gideon Welles

The Union tried to blockade all the Southern ports, but Confederate ships still slipped past them to the open sea. They were called *blockade-runners*. These ships would leave their ports at night. They would sail to Nassau in the Bahamas, where their precious cargoes of cotton would be unloaded and sold. The profits would be used to buy clothing, foods, and equipment. These supplies were brought back into a Southern port using the same daring technique.

Great Britain was sympathetic to the Southern cause. The country built and sold blockade-running ships to the Confederacy. These ships were built with low sides. They had **rigging** for sails and a steam-powered paddle wheel. They were also built with a light draft, which meant they could navigate in shallow waters. It allowed them to slip past the Union blockading ships that required more water to operate.

The captains and crew of these blockade-runners came from all walks of life. Successful trips could be very profitable and well worth the risk.

The blockade-runners were fairly successful, especially in the early stages of the war. In the beginning, there were many open Southern ports and few blockaders. But as the ports of the South began to fall, the situation became more and more hopeless.

The last port fell in January 1865. General Robert E. Lee's army was eventually forced to surrender due to a lack of food and war materials. This happened on April 9, 1865, at Appomattox Courthouse in Virginia.

The Appomattox Courthouse

Confederate Cruisers

Another Southern plan was designed to weaken the North's international trade. The Confederacy organized about 20 commerce raiders. These Confederate cruisers attacked Union **merchant** ships.

In the course of the Civil War, commerce raiders destroyed 257 Union merchant ships. They also forced more than 700 other Union ships to travel under foreign flags to avoid attack. Even so, these

Robert E. Lee

Raphael Semmes, captain of the C.S.S. *Alabama*

Merchant Marine

The merchant marine is a group of privately or publicly owned business ships. The ships carry cargo and passengers. A country may call on these ships to help out during wartime. Merchant marine officers are the men and women who operate the ships.

To learn more about navy vessels, check out this online dictionary of American Naval Fighting Ships.
http://www.hazegray.org/danfs/

raiders had little effect on the outcome of the war. They did, however, manage to disrupt Northern trade and nearly destroy the United States Merchant Marine.

The C.S.S. *Alabama* was the most famous commerce raider. Raphael Semmes was the captain of this paddle wheel cruiser. This steamship carried ten cannons. It destroyed or captured a total of 64 Northern merchant ships, plus one federal warship. It was eventually sunk in a ship-to-ship duel with the U.S.S. *Kearsarge* off the French coast.

Ironclads

When Virginia seceded from the Union in April of 1861, the Confederacy demanded the surrender of the U.S. Navy yard at Norfolk. Before giving it up, the Union commander ordered that the yard be burned and the ships sunk in the shallow Elizabeth River.

The C.S.S. *Virginia*

The Confederate secretary of the navy was Stephen Mallory. He knew that England and France had tried putting iron on the sides of their wooden ships for protection. In order to keep the Southern ports opened against the blockade, he ordered that a special ironclad ship be built. It would be powered by steam and have a large number of powerful guns. It could then safely destroy the Union's wooden blockading ships.

Mallory had the U.S.S. *Merrimac* raised from the bottom of the Elizabeth River and put in **dry dock**. For about a year, 1,500 men worked on this ship. They applied tons of iron plates to the ship. This took a long time because the Confederacy was not an industrial nation. Next, they fixed the engines and installed eight broadside guns and a **bow** and **stern** gun. A metal ram was built on its **prow** that could sink wooden warships. The Confederates called this new ironclad the C.S.S. *Virginia*.

The *Merrimac* before (above) and after (below) it became an ironclad

On March 8, 1862, the new C.S.S. *Virginia* moved slowly down the Elizabeth River. The sun glistened on the pork fat on her slanted sides. The slippery grease would make it harder for enemies to board the ship. It would also help deflect cannon balls.

The ironclad met the Union wooden ships at Hampton Roads, a channel that empties into Chesapeake Bay. It destroyed two Northern ships and grounded three others. In these battles, Union cannonballs harmlessly bounced off the *Virginia*.

Battle between the *Monitor* and the *Merrin*

The ironclad returned the next day to finish the job. It faced the U.S.S. *Monitor*, an ironclad ship designed especially for the Northern navy. This ship was a low-freeboard steamship with a small number of heavy guns in a turret. "Low-freeboard" means the deck of the ship was very close to the water. A turret is an armored box that rotates to aim the guns. The *Monitor* was often called a "cheese box on a raft."

In history's first battle between ironclad warships, neither side won. But the *Monitor* did prevent the *Virginia* from destroying the remaining Union ships at Hampton Roads. Later, the U.S. Navy built a large ironclad fleet designed after the *Monitor*.

Pook Turtles

At the time of the Civil War, the Mississippi and its streams were the highways of the West. Good north-south roads did not exist, and there were few railroads. Northern control of these rivers would deprive the South of beef and grain and good fighting men from the western states. To gain control of these rivers, the Union established an inland navy. It was sometimes referred to as the "Brown Water Navy."

Samuel Pook designed ironclads for this navy. These ironclads became known as "Pook Turtles." They were made from flat-bottomed boats 175 feet long and nearly 52 feet wide. A single paddle wheel was set into the stern.

A casemate, or armored box, held the paddle wheel, engines, and guns. Each ship mounted three powerful guns pointing forward, four smaller weapons in each broadside, and two light guns aimed backward.

The ships were expected to fight head-on. Only the front part of the casemate and the sides protecting the boilers and engines had a metal covering. The stern and a large part of the sides were unarmored. Since they were powered by steam, they had to be constantly refueled from coal **barges**.

The Confederacy used many of its ironclads to defend their harbors and rivers. The Union used its ironclads to fight the Southern ironclads and to bombard Southern forts and land forces. These Pook Turtles helped General Grant's Union army win the battles at Fort Henry, Fort Donelson, and Vicksburg. They played an important role in the Union gaining complete control of the Mississippi River and eventually winning the war.

The ironclads were some of the first ships in history to be armored with metal and propelled by steam. This development led directly to today's ships. The ironclads were the great-grandparents of modern warships.

The Battle of Mobile Bay

The Confederacy designed new weapons to destroy the ships in the Union blockade.

Submarines

The South built the first submarine used successfully in warfare. The H.L. *Hunley* was a 40-foot-long iron war vessel. A harpoon torpedo was mounted on the bow. It could be driven into a wooden **hull** of an enemy ship. Then the H.L. *Hunley* could back away and explode the **charge** from a safe distance.

On its first attack on February 17, 1864, the H.L. *Hunley* rammed a Union warship with the harpoon torpedo. The resulting explosion sent the Union ship to the bottom. However, on its return trip, the nine-man submarine mysteriously sank, losing the entire crew.

Torpedo Service

The Confederates also created the Torpedo Service. Mines were placed in Southern waterways and harbors to defend against Union warships. These mines, called *torpedoes*, came in many sizes and shapes. They contained charges that exploded on contact with a vessel's hull or by remote control from shore. Because of poor waterproofing, many torpedoes misfired. These mines still managed to sink or damage 43 Union ships, including 4 powerful monitors.

Mobile Bay

By the summer of 1864, the Union blockade had closed all but two Confederate ports. Mobile Bay in Alabama was the last Confederate port in the Gulf of Mexico. The Union needed to close this port and stop the remaining blockade-runners.

David Glasgow Farragut had been promoted to rear admiral for taking New Orleans and helping General Grant take Vicksburg. This had given the Union complete control of the Mississippi River. But Admiral Farragut knew that taking Mobile Bay would not be easy.

A row of sunken **pilings** and a field of mines narrowed the bay's entrance. Ships entering the bay would have to pass in front of Fort Morgan's 47 guns. This huge brick fort had guns powerful enough to blast large holes in Farragut's wooden ships. And if his fleet made it safely past *this* fort, they would face a Confederate **flotilla** led by the C.S.S. *Tennessee*. This powerful ironclad ram was shaped like the C.S.S. *Virginia* but had thicker iron plates. It also had rifled guns, which could shoot farther.

Farragut had 14 wooden ships and 4 small ironclad monitors. This fleet began the attack on Mobile Bay on the morning of August 5, 1864. A land army force supported them.

The admiral had the four monitors take the lead. They could stay close to shore, protected from the fort's guns. The wooden ships were behind and to the left of the monitors.

Farragut ordered the smaller ships lashed to the port side of the larger ships. The larger ships would fight Fort Morgan with their starboard broadsides. This way, the smaller ships could tow the larger ones if they were damaged in battle.

Ulysses S. Grant

Farragut's ships steamed into the narrow passage in front of Fort Morgan. Then a Union mistake nearly resulted in a Confederate victory. The leading monitor, U.S.S. *Tecumseh*, struck a torpedo and sank in a matter of minutes. In a state of confusion, the fleet came to a halt in front of the powerful guns of Fort Morgan. The wooden ships took a terrible pounding from the fort and from the four Confederate ships just inside the bay.

On the U.S.S. *Hartford*, shot after shot came through the side, mowing down the men. An eyewitness reported that the deck became slippery with blood and body parts. The dead were dragged to the port side of the ship. The wounded were sent below for medical care.

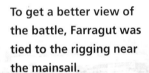

To get a better view of the battle, Farragut was tied to the rigging near the mainsail.

Surrender of the C.S.S. *Tennessee* at the Battle of Mobile Bay

Then the captain of the U.S.S. *Brooklyn* signaled back to Farragut, "Torpedoes ahead!" Not wanting to remain under Fort Morgan's guns, Admiral Farragut shouted back, "Full speed ahead!"

The U.S.S. *Hartford* passed by the U.S.S. *Brooklyn* and moved into the minefield. Its guns blazed at Fort Morgan. Sailors below the deck on the U.S.S. *Hartford* heard the ship's hull bumping against torpedoes. None of the mines exploded though. The rest of Farragut's ships made it through, but some were badly damaged.

Once inside the bay, the wooden ships separated. Soon they defeated the Confederate flotilla. After an unsuccessful attempt to sink the U.S.S. *Hartford*, even the C.S.S. *Tennessee* was forced to surrender. The constant attack from Farragut's wooden ships and monitors had damaged the ship. It could not be steered and was disabled. Eventually, all of Mobile Bay fell into Union hands. It was one of the most decisive naval victories in the Civil War.

Powder Monkeys

During the Civil War, young boys served on navy warships. Their most important job was being powder monkeys. *Monkey* was a sailor's term that applied to any small object.

During a battle, these boys were responsible for keeping their assigned deck guns supplied with gunpowder. It was a very dangerous job. Upon receiving an order, they would hurry to the magazine, the part of a ship that safely stored gunpowder. A woolen screen soaked with water would usually hang before its entrance. The screen had a hole in it so the powder monkeys could pick up a premade cannon charge. They placed the charge in a leather pouch and quickly returned it to their cannon crew. These precautions were taken to prevent the gunpowder from accidentally exploding.

Sailors on the deck of the gunboat *Hunchback*

Powder monkeys had the rank of third class boy, second class boy, or first class boy. Their rank and pay depended on their age, size, and qualifications. The boys weren't paid until they were discharged, except for a small amount for clothing and spending money. During the Civil War, it was possible for powder monkeys to enlist for a one-year term of service.

There were certain requirements for becoming a powder monkey in the Union navy. Boys, ages 13 through 17, needed written permission from a parent or guardian. No boy could have a physical disability, be in poor health, or have a criminal conviction. No candidate who could not spell, write clearly, or do simple math problems was accepted. Each boy also had to be at least 4 feet 8 inches tall.

In both the North and the South, new recruits were sent to receiving ships at navy yards. These old sail-powered ships became the training grounds and dorms for future powder monkeys. Union receiving ships were located in Boston, New York, Norfolk, and other cities.

While aboard a receiving ship, the boys learned the basics of navy life. They also learned about uniforms, rigging, different kinds of boats, and how to handle sails.

The length of time aboard the receiving ship depended on the needs of the regular navy. It could be a few days to a few weeks. Anything not learned aboard the receiving ship had to be learned in active service.

Once assigned to a warship, these boys were under the charge of the master-at-arms. When not serving as powder monkeys during a battle, the boys had to perform other duties.

After the war, the U.S. gunboat *Hunchback* was sold to the New York and Brooklyn Ferry Company. It was renamed *General Grant* in honor of Ulysses S. Grant. The boat remained in service until 1880.

A Badge
of Courage

On December 21, 1861, President Abraham Lincoln signed into law the navy Medal of Honor for bravery in action. On July 12, 1862, he signed into law the Medal of Honor for the army. Although it was created for the Civil War, Congress made the Medal of Honor a permanent honor in 1863. The Congressional Medal of Honor is the highest award for courage in action against an enemy force that can be given to an individual serving in the armed services.

Steam-powered ships required refueling from coal barges. This was a dirty operation. So boys had to help holystone the decks and help polish the ship's brass fixtures, called the *brightworks*. Some were assigned as messenger boys for officers. Others performed regular maintenance on the lines and sails.

Gun crews on warships ate together. Powder boys from these mess crews were chosen to be the cook's assistant for a week. Their duty was to bring the food to the table and serve it to their crew.

Boys from the North and the South also served in the inland navy. They fought battles along the Mississippi River. Boys were assigned to Southern ironclads or Northern Pook Turtles. They were often called "brown water powder monkeys."

Many powder monkeys were killed or severely wounded in the Civil War. Several received the Medal of Honor for their courage.

AFTERWORD

The modern United States, with its government, laws, and people, is a product of the Civil War. More than 100 million black and white Americans living today have ancestors who were directly affected by the war. Either they fought in the war, were freed from slavery, or were forced to free their slaves. This war shaped their lives, their society, and their nation. Through them, the Civil War shaped future generations of Americans.

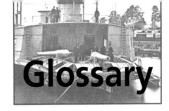

Glossary

admiral	commander in chief of a navy
barge	boat that carries things
berth	place to sit or sleep on a ship
bible	chunk of sandstone that was the size of a Bible
blockade	the shutting off of a place (as by warships) to prevent people or supplies from getting through
blockade-runner	ship or person that runs through a blockade (see separate entry for *blockade*)
boiler	tank in which hot water is stored or water is heated
bow	forward or front part of a ship
broadsides	firing of all the guns on one side of a ship at the same time
bulwarks	side of a ship above the upper deck
channel	narrow sea between two bodies of land
charge	load of explosives
Confederacy	Southern side during the Civil War
discharge	release from duty or service
dry dock	dock that is kept dry for the repairing of ships
flagship	ship that carries the commander of the fleet
fleet	group of ships under a single command
flotilla	fleet of ships (see separate entry for *fleet*)

hatch	opening in the deck of a ship
holystoned	scrubbed with Bible-sized chunks of sandstone
hull	frame or body of a ship
Industrial Revolution	period in U.S. history when the use of machines replaced human labor
ironclad	covered with iron for protection
magazine	room where powder and other explosives are kept on a ship
maneuvers	military or naval actions
marines	soldiers serving on a ship
mast	long pole rising from the deck of a ship that supports the sail
master-at-arms	officer in charge of discipline on a ship
masthead	top of a mast (see separate entry for *mast*)
merchant	relating to the buying and selling of products
mess	food or meal
Mess Bill	list of kitchen jobs
monitor	warship covered with heavy protection (usually metal)
muster	meeting of troops to take attendance and receive orders
navy	branch of the military that fights on bodies of water using warships
pilings	heavy beams of wood, concrete, or steel driven into the ground that ships can't sail over

port	left side of a ship
powder monkey	boy in the navy who was responsible for keeping his assigned deck guns supplied with gunpowder
prow	forward or front part of a ship; bow
rail	light structure serving as a guard at the edge of a ship's deck
ram	warship with a pointed front end for piercing an enemy ship
Rebs	Rebels; soldiers fighting on the Confederate side of the war
reveille	bugle call signaling the beginning of the day
rigging	lines and chains used to support sails
sailcloth	heavy material used for sails
scuttlebutt	rumor or gossip
secession	act of leaving the Union
sheet chains	chains that control the angle of the sails
sponger	person who sponges out the barrel of a cannon after it's been fired
starboard	right side of a ship
steersmen	men who steer a ship
stern	rear of a boat
tattoo	call sounded as notice to go to quarters (room on a ship)
tug	strong boat used to tow or push other boats
Union	Northern side during the Civil War

Index